The Monkey and the Fishermen
with
The Donkey in the Pond

Illustrated by Val Biro

Award Publications Limited

Once there was a monkey who lived high up in a palm tree by a river.

He liked this palm tree best because he loved to eat its juicy coconuts and drink their milk.

One day he looked into the river and saw a plump fish poke its head out of the water.

"I love coconuts, but I wish I knew how to catch fish, too," he thought.

Just then, two men came along the riverbank. They were carrying a large, heavy net.

"I wonder what that is for?" thought the monkey. "I will watch to see what happens."

The men were fishermen. The monkey watched closely as they tied their net across the river.

"We should catch lots of fish today," said one man. Then off they went to wait in the shade.

The monkey jumped down from his tree. "Now I know how to catch fish," he said, "I shall try to catch one myself."

He found an old net in the fishermen's hut nearby.

The net was very heavy, but the monkey dragged it down to the riverbank.

He tied one end to a branch, then jumped into the water.

But the poor monkey could not swim.

He got tangled up in the net.
"Help me!" he cried.

Just then, the fishermen came back. They were surprised to find the monkey caught in one of their nets.

"It takes time to learn to catch fish," they said, as they helped the monkey out of the water.

The monkey ran back to his tree. "From now on I will stick to catching coconuts," he said.

The Donkey in the Pond

One hot day a farmer was leading his donkey home from market. The farmer was happy.

But the donkey was sad. He carried heavy sacks full of salt. It was hard work in the heat of the sun.

The poor donkey struggled on. Suddenly he slipped on the rough path and fell into a pond. *Splash*!

The farmer was angry. All his salt had washed away. But the donkey was happy now that his load was lighter.

The next day it was even hotter. The farmer bought lots of sponges from the market.
Once again, the donkey was unhappy with his load.

Remembering what had happened the day before, the donkey threw himself into the pond. This time the farmer just smiled.

The donkey did not know that the sponges would fill up with water. Now his load was much heavier! "Silly donkey!" said the farmer.